Pathfinder 34

Words:
teaching and learning vocabulary

The *Pathfinder* Series

Active learning — listening and reading

Reading for pleasure in a foreign language (PF2)
Ann Swarbrick   ISBN 0 948003 98 7

Developing skills for independent reading (PF22)
Iain Mitchell & Ann Swarbrick   ISBN 1 874016 34 8

Creative use of texts (PF21)
Bernard Kavanagh & Lynne Upton   ISBN 1 874016 28 3

Listening in a foreign language (PF26)
A skill we take for granted?
Karen Turner   ISBN 1 874016 44 5

Stimulating grammatical awareness (PF33)
A fresh look at language acquisition
Heather Rendall   ISBN 1 902031 08 3

Supporting learners and learning

Teaching learners how to learn
Strategy training in the ML classroom (PF31)
Vee Harris   ISBN 1 874016 83 6

Making effective use of the dictionary (PF28)
Gwen Berwick and Phil Horsfall   ISBN 1 874016 60 7

Nightshift (PF20)
Ideas and strategies for homework
David Buckland & Mike Short   ISBN 1 874016 19 4

Grammar matters (PF17)
Susan Halliwell   ISBN 1 874016 12 7

Planning and organising teaching

Assessment and planning in the MFL department (PF29)
Harmer Parr   ISBN 1 874016 71 2

Departmental planning and schemes of work (PF11)
Clive Hurren   ISBN 1 874016 10 0

Fair enough? (PF14)
Equal opportunities and modern languages
Vee Harris   ISBN 1 874016 03 8

Foreign Language Assistants (PF32)
A guide to good practice
*David Rowles, Marian Carty
and Anneli McLachlan*   ISBN 1 874016 95 X

Bridging the gap (PF7)
GCSE to 'A' level
John Thorogood & Lid King   ISBN 0 948003 89 8

Improve your image (PF15)
The effective use of the OHP
Daniel Tierney & Fay Humphreys   ISBN 1 874016 04 6

Teaching/learning in the target language

On target (PF5)
Teaching in the target language
Susan Halliwell & Barry Jones   ISBN 0 948003 54 5

Keeping on target (PF23)
Bernardette Holmes   ISBN 1 874016 35 5

Motivating all learners

Yes — but will they behave? (PF4)
Managing the interactive classroom
Susan Halliwell   ISBN 0 948003 44 8

Not bothered? (PF16)
Motivating reluctant language learners in Key Stage 4
Jenifer Alison   ISBN 1 874016 06 2

Communication re-activated (PF6)
Teaching pupils with learning difficulties
Bernardette Holmes   ISBN 0 948003 59 6

Differentiation (PF18)
Taking the initiative
Anne Convery & Do Coyle   ISBN 1 874016 18 6

Cultural awareness

Crossing frontiers (PF30)
The school study visit abroad
David Snow & Michael Byram   ISBN 1 874016 84 4

Languages home and away (PF9)
Alison Taylor   ISBN 0 948003 84 7

Exploring otherness (PF24)
An approach to cultural awareness
Barry Jones   ISBN 1 874016 42 9

Broadening the learning experience

New contexts for modern language learning (PF27)
Cross-curricular approaches
Kim Brown & Margot Brown   ISBN 1 874016 50 X

With a song in my scheme of work (PF25)
Steven Fawkes   ISBN 1 874016 45 3

Drama in the languages classroom (PF19)
Judith Hamilton & Anne McLeod   ISBN 1 874016 07 0

Being Creative (PF10)
Barry Jones   ISBN 0 948003 99 5

All Pathfinders are available through good book suppliers or direct from **Grantham Book Services,** Isaac Newton Way, Alma Park Industrial Estate, Grantham, Lincs NG31 9SD.
Fax orders to: 01476 541 061. Credit card orders: 01476 541 080

Pathfinder 34

A CILT series for language teachers

Words

Teaching and learning vocabulary

David Snow

CILT
Centre for Information
on Language Teaching and Research

Acknowledgements

I should like to thank the following who have contributed to this volume:

My wife, Alison, and Michael Byram who read the text and offered useful suggestions. Val Seaward and the staff of St Bede's school, Lanchester, Lynn Powell and the staff of Farringdon school, Sunderland. Katrin Fœrster, Isabelle Ledez, Antonia Estèvez-Blanca and Victoria McGuiness who helped with suggestions for examples in German, French and Spanish.

First published 1998
Copyright © 1998 Centre for Information on Language Teaching and Research
ISBN 1 902031 14 8

A catalogue record for this book is available from the British Library
Printed in Great Britain by Copyprint UK Ltd

Published by the Centre for Information on Language Teaching and Research,
20 Bedfordbury, Covent Garden, London WC2N 4LB

CILT Publications are available from: Grantham Book Services, Isaac Newton Way, Alma Park Industrial Estate, Grantham, Lincs NG31 8SD. Tel: 01476 541 080. Fax: 01476 541 061. Book trade representation (UK and Ireland): Broadcast Book Services, 24 De Montfort Road, London SW16 1LZ. Tel: 0181 677 5129.

Contents

Introduction

Words
which are 'taught'. . .

&

Words
which are 'caught'

There are basically two ways of 'getting' new vocabulary:

(i) **conscious learning** of specific words which have been 'taught' by the teacher; and
(ii) sub-conscious **absorption** of words as they crop up incidentally.

Several studies into the acquisition of vocabulary have demonstrated how few words are actually retained from those which are 'learned' or 'taught' by direct instruction. On the other hand, various researchers have concluded that for most proficient speakers of other languages by far the largest part of their vocabulary has been 'caught' in the second way. This is also borne out by the reflections of speakers of other languages themselves.

It is surprising, therefore, that in recent years teachers have tended to become locked into the first of the two ways of providing opportunities for their learners to 'get' new vocabulary, at the expense of the second. Because there is a definite gap between what is 'taught' and what is 'learned' more attention needs to be paid to 'getting' vocabulary incidentally.

The intention of this book is to reflect critically, in the light of the above points, on the following issues:

*   what vocabulary should be taught and how it should be taught;
*   how vocabulary might be more focused on specific needs;
*   techniques and strategies which are already in use;
*   the extent to which some older language learning activities might be revived to improve vocabulary learning;
*   some idiosyncratic methods of rapidly expanding the learners' stock of vocabulary;
*   the additional options created by new technologies for effectively facilitating language acquisition by **absorption** within the classroom and home context;
*   the contribution of the study of words to the **language awareness** and **cultural** aims of the National Curriculum.

1.　The teacher's viewpoint

PLANNING

The problem with synonyms is that there aren't any! Before the advent of the National Curriculum the words on the right were generally considered more or less synonymous in foreign language learning, as they are in common usage. They were understood in vague

terms and were matters which teachers had in their sub-conscious mind, without any one of them having a direct influence on the day-to-day life of the classroom.

The Non-statutory Guidance of the National Curriculum made explicit the ways in which these words should be used in MFL teaching, with distinct and specific meanings. In the field of vocabulary learning (as well as in other aspects of language learning) it is essential that any discussion of approaches to teaching should put these three words at the centre of planning schemes of work, units of work and individual lessons:

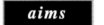 **goals**

Yet the requirements of the original National Curriculum were so complex that this central issue was submerged in a superfluity of detailed practical suggestions.

The business of ensuring that the National Curriculum requirements are covered is often left to the writers of the textbook. However, textbook writers may be influenced by matters that blur the focus of classroom activities (what is enjoyable, what can be presented in a visually interesting way, what the graphics designer finds attractive, etc.) This puts the onus on the teacher to make the connection between an entitlement to a particular opportunity and the objectives and goals of the current Unit of Work.

It is for the above reasons that the following interpretation of the definitions of the aims, objectives and goals is offered here. It is not intended to replace what is said in the Non-statutory Guidance, but rather to emphasise the importance of this matter when considering vocabulary teaching and learning.

CILT

aims

can be expressed under four headings:

- communicative competence;
- language awareness;
- cultural awareness;
- general learning skills.

objectives

are the specific ways in which the teacher gears his/her teaching towards one or more of the above aims. Objectives should be expressed in terms of what the pupils should be able to do or should know by the end of a unit or by the end of a particular lesson.

Examples
- be able to express an opinion about a matter of personal interest (a function objective, linked to the communication aim);
- be able to write a few sentences about a recent experience (a grammatical objective, linked to the communication aim);
- know that there are three kinds of secondary school in Germany; or
- know that many French children think that wearing school uniforms is strange (knowledge objectives, linked to the cultural awareness aim);
- use a dictionary and identify the gender of a noun (metalanguage objective, linked to the language awareness aim);
- learn a text for a play (a language objective linked to general learning/memorising aim).

goals

are what the teacher presents to the pupils as a reason for a lesson or unit and should reflect the aims and objectives of the teacher. It is the *goals* that will mean most to the pupils so they should be **realistic, interesting, enjoyable, stimulating and challenging.**

Examples:
- a project (e.g. individual, group or whole class entry for a competition);
- a product (e.g. a wall display, making a cassette to send to a linked school);
- a process (e.g. reading or listening extensively for pleasure and/or to extend vocabulary acquisition);
- an experience (e.g. a trip abroad, or work experience, preparing to receive a group).

Most lessons should be presented within the context of these *goals*. Only the brightest, most well motivated pupils will react positively to the sort of language learning which is directly linked to what they perceive as vague and irrelevant *aims* and *objectives*. The *goals* provide the very important factor in learning of instant gratification.

WHAT VOCABULARY TO INCLUDE IN A UNIT OF WORK OR A LESSON

The specific vocabulary to be 'learned' may come from:

- the textbook writer; or
- an examination syllabus; or
- a frequency list which exists for all the commonly taught languages.

What often happens is that learning a list of words from one of the above sources is seen as an objective in itself. An inordinate amount of time can be spent on studying and practising a comprehensive list of vocabulary which is of doubtful use, or at least which only has limited use within one or two skill areas.

Before teaching pupils a particular selection of words the teacher should really make judgements about these questions:

- What is the appropriate selection of vocabulary pupils will need to achieve the current **goal?**
- Will they need to 'know' this vocabulary for **receptive** purposes or for **productive** purposes?
- If receptive, does that mean understanding both the **spoken** words and the **written** words?
- If productive, will the ability to use the words in speaking **and** in writing be equally important?

In the initial planning stage there should be a judgement made about the body of words to be learned in terms of the above questions. It is true that learning for one purpose probably helps learning for another and learning words for productive use will not be possible if they cannot first be used receptively. However, the teacher can be unduly influenced by the textbook where the distinction is seldom expressed and where too often the reason for the inclusion of a group of words is related less to the current goal than to the fact that they lead to entertaining activities or can be attractively illustrated in the book.

For example, the topic of 'Weather' will generally be tackled from the angle of a traditional collection of verb phrases to be learned, as found in most courses:

Figure 1

English	Español	Français	Deutsch
What's the weather like?	¿Qué tiempo hace?	Quel temps fait-il?	Wie ist das Wetter?
It's hot	Hace calor	Il fait chaud	Es ist warm
It's cold	Hace frío	Il fait froid	Es ist kalt
It's fine	Hace buen tiempo	Il fait beau	Es ist sonnig
It's poor weather	Hace mal tiempo	Il fait mauvais	Es ist schlechtes Wetter
It's raining	Llueve	Il pleut	Es regnet
It's snowing	Nieva	Il neige	Es schneit
It's hailing	Graniza	Il grêle	Es hagelt
It's freezing	Hiela	Il gèle	Es friert
It's foggy	Hay niebla	Il fait du brouillard	Es ist nebelig
It's windy	Hace viento	Il fait du vent	Es ist windig

Admittedly, this is all very neat and tidy and it is certainly true that the aspect of vocabulary learning which involves thinking about how to organise words into groups is useful. However, young learners are unlikely to be in situations where they will frequently need all the above vocabulary, either when speaking or when writing. Even the need to **recognise** the words when they are spoken or written by someone else is less than the time spent on 'learning' them would suggest.

Under the topic of 'Weather', it would be more useful to start from the pupils' angle, with the question: 'Which words will I need to know to reach this particular goal?'

The goal will be expressed in one or more of the following sorts of ways:

By the end of this Unit we will be able to:
a) understand a weather forecast on the television; or
b) understand a weather forecast on the radio; or
c) understand when our partner class is talking about the weather in their area (on tape, on video); or
d) understand a weather forecast in the newspaper; or
e) tell our partner class (on tape/in writing?) about what sort of weather they are likely to experience here when they visit us.

An analysis of the vocabulary needed to achieve these goals will provide us with a list of words which is somewhat different from those in the traditional list (*Figure 1*). The words needed to achieve the first of the goals suggested above will be more like the list in *Figure 2*, below.

Figure 2

English	Español	Français	Deutsch
Rain	Nuboso	Pluie	Regen
Showers	Cielos cubiertos/	Neige	Sonnenschein
Sunshine	despejados	Brouillard	Nebel
Sunny periods	Tormentas	Tempêtes	Schnee
Fog	Viento fuerte	Vents forts/faibles	Kaltwetterfront
Snow	El norte/el sur/	Soleil (sur la région	Warmwetterfront
Wind	el este/el oeste	parisienne/sur la moitié	windig stürmisch
Bright intervals	1–40 grados	nord du pays)	Hagel
Storms . . . in the	bajo cero	Les différentes régions	kalt/warm . . . im Süden
north/south/east/west	Soleado	Vous aurez besoin d'un	. . . Norden . . . Osten
High/Low pressure	Borrasca	parapluie/	. . . Westen
Higher/lower than	Anticiclón	d'un manteau/d'un	hoher Luftdruck,
normal temperatures	Lluvias fuertes/débiles	gros pull	niedriger Luftdruck

Furthermore, if the selection of vocabulary to be studied is made in this way, the learning can be much more focused, and perhaps more effective than if the teacher tries to cover all four language skills with every new word.

For the goals (a), (b) or (c) above, the words needed will be for **aural comprehension only**. The practical teaching consequence of this is that within this particular context there can be a much greater concentration on listening than when there is a perceived need to practise all four skills for all new vocabulary. The teacher may be able to set more demanding tasks and use more authentic material than is usually the case.

If the goal is as in (d) above then the main thrust of the teaching at this stage would be the **reading** skill, and in particular the ability to scan a text for information.

It would only be if the unit goal involved **writing** or **speaking** as in (e) above that the traditional selection of vocabulary might be as important as the words in *Figure 2* and even then appropriate parts of the verbs in two or three different tenses might be more relevant to needs than a comprehensive range of weather possibilities.

In *Figure 3* there are some suggestions about beginning to construct a list of vocabulary to be taught for the specific goal of writing a letter or sending a tape to a partnership

CiLT

class, in which one of the tasks would be to talk about the weather during their last holiday, or what it will be like when their visitors come next week, for example.

Figure 3

English	Español	Français	Deutsch
I hope it's not going to rain. It's always foggy at this time of the year. It should be fine when you arrive.	Hemos tenido un tiempo muy bueno, mucho sol aunque por la noche ha hecho frío. Espero que siga este tiempo tan agradable.	Nous avons eu un hiver effroyable. Il a plu pendant tout le mois d'avril. J'espère qu'il fera beau pendant ton séjour.	Wie war das Wetter? Das Wetter war (einfach) herrlich/ angenehm/furchtbar. Es war richtiges Frühlingswetter/ Sommerwetter/ Herbstwetter/ Winterwetter.

If the vocabulary is chosen for a written purpose such as this, more intensive and demanding written work can be done with the learners than when the teacher is trying to teach all four skills.

Other 'traditional' vocabulary lists might be examined from the same point of view. What is the purpose, for example, of pupils 'learning' (i.e. learning how to spell) all the parts of the body, all items of clothing or food, the names of all the pets, etc? How often does anyone have to use the written form of numbers (apart from 1–10)?

If the type of learning of new vocabulary is made more selective, as proposed above, there will be more room in the classroom and at home for extensive reading and listening which are so often neglected for 'lack of time'. These are the activities which will provide learners with the opportunity to extend their vocabulary by sub-conscious acquisition rather than by 'learning' lists.

It could be rightly argued that what is suggested in terms of a re-think in attitudes towards lists of vocabulary to be learnt is an overwhelming task and not one for the individual teacher. However, the proposal here is a more modest one: simply to reduce the amount of time spent on learning lists, in order to allow more time for other things. For those who might wish to pursue the idea of developing a critical attitude towards lists, there is a suggestion on p50 about using post-16 learners in the process.

'LEARN THE NEW VOCABULARY FOR HOMEWORK'

It is certainly each teacher's prerogative to use whatever tools, strategies or activities have been found to work — and setting vocabulary learning as a homework task is certainly one of the traditional *'things to do'* when teaching languages. However, the complaint is often to be heard that 'they won't/don't do their homework, particularly when it's learning' so it is perhaps worthwhile to discuss the reasons for this and to re-assess whether the activity is useful and, if so, whether it can be made more effective. If the instruction 'Learn the new vocabulary for homework' is to have productive results in language learning, it is worth considering our *objectives* when we give the instruction and then to make sure that the pupils have the same perception and understanding of what is required.

The learning of vocabulary for homework may be appropriate in schools where the tradition of homework is well established and the teacher can be sure that an instruction to 'learn the new words for homework' will be understood:

- the teacher will have taught the skills of memorising (and will remind them before each 'learning' homework how to go about it (see Chapter 10);
- she will have a clear picture of the way in which the new words fit into her objectives and scheme of work and will make sure that the pupils see the learning in terms of the current unit **goal;**
- she will be clear in her own mind whether the vocabulary to be learned will be needed for receptive or productive use.

When the learning has been undertaken, the teacher needs to weigh up the advantage of testing (just to show whether or not they have done what they were told) against the time taken for the test which might be more effectively spent on practising, reinforcing and using the new words in context.

If the learning **is** followed by a test, the test should reflect the objectives of the teacher and should not automatically be a question of pupils having to supply TL equivalents, correctly spelt, of English words.

TESTING EACH OTHER

An alternative to the written test is a regular five-minute session when the pupils test each other orally in pairs (see Appendix B). If it is pointed out to the pupils that one of the best ways of learning is by teaching, both sides of the testing-tested partnerships will

CILT

have a motivation to get on with the job. The sense that people feel when faced with a test is not that their knowledge is being checked, but that they are being tested as people. When pair-testing is going on there can be a real sense of helping each other to learn.

 ## ALTERNATIVES TO 'LEARN THE NEW WORDS FOR HOMEWORK'

There are more specific homework tasks for reinforcing new vocabulary which pupils find more motivating than the vague **'learn for a test'** approach. If the teacher has decided that the emphasis for a particular group of words must be on the form of the words, or **spelling,** the following **strategies for reinforcing** them are worth considering. The principles can be adapted for use with near beginners or advanced learners.

- Write sentences, each including one of the new words, in such a way as to show the meaning of the word.
- On a sheet of paper write a sentence using each of the new words. Put the new words in pencil. When you have finished, rub out the 'new' words and we will see if others in the class can put in the correct words tomorrow. (You will need to remember what you have put, so that you can check what other people think!)
- Write a definition of each of the new words.
- Write some anagrams which we will try on each other tomorrow. You will need to be able to judge whether or not your friends get the right answer!
- Write a word-search including the new words. We will try this on other people within the next few days.

In all these cases, the focus is on learning the **form** or **spelling** of the words which, as we have seen, is not always the teacher's objective. When it is, however:

- each of the suggested tasks has a purpose which pupils can see and is likely to be more motivating than a simple instruction to 'learn the new words for homework'; and
- all of them require a particular effort of thought, rather than simple memorising.

2. The pupil's viewpoint

Before any **meaningful** learning will take place, the pupil needs to know the answers to the following five questions:

 'WHY DO I NEED TO LEARN THESE PARTICULAR WORDS?'

In the first column are the answers he or she may be given or may deduce from the teacher's attitude. In the second column are the ways the cynical, or over-loaded pupil might see it and in the third column is a comment for reflection.

Why learn these words?	A reasonable reaction	*Food for thought*
The teacher says so.	I will do as I'm told: I have faith in what s/he says	*An admirable sentiment, but alas not universal!*
Research suggests that we need to hear/see new words up to twelve times before we remember them.	Well, I'll never learn this language then!	*Perhaps, this is one of those pieces of information which is best kept to ourselves and remembered in our planning?*
They are in the book.	I'm not interested. Books are boring.	*Has the writer of the textbook hit the right level for the pupils in terms of realism, interest, fun, intellectual challenge and stimulation?*
They are in the GCSE syllabus.	The GCSE is years away. OR I'm fed up hearing about the GCSE.	*Is it the teacher's job to add to the anxiety about examinations and the sense of boredom and tiredness they can create?*
These are 'general purpose' words; they are needed for everything we want to say or write or understand in the FL.	Such words will be met frequently any way, so what is so special about learning them at home instead of in class?	*Yes, perhaps more focused learning or listening or reading would be a better use of their time?*
These words will be necessary if we are to achieve (the **goal**) of this lesson or unit.	An excellent reason to spend some time on them.	*If the learning is focused on the present needs, which are the skills which should be practised?*

CiLT

'WHAT DO YOU MEAN, LEARN?'

On the left are the teacher's possible objectives. On the right are points for reflection:

Objective	Can this be achieved by a 'learning' homework?
To recognise the words when you *see* them.	Yes. Are the pupils aware that this is the teacher's only objective? Do they know how to go about learning for this purpose?
To recognise the words when you *hear* them.	Maybe (if they have been well practised in class, first). Perhaps the more able can do this by the end of the lesson anyway. Will the less well motivated spend the time wisely?
To use the words *to talk about* . . . (whatever is the current **goal**)	Not unless they have already started along this road in class.
To use them when you *write about* . . . (the current **goal**)	
To be able to *translate* from English into the TL.	Yes — but is this really an objective when we profess to be trying to get our learners to think in the TL?
All the above or not specified.	A very complicated matter for pupils to deal with, without clear guidance.

'HOW DO WE LEARN?'

This is not a question which will often be posed by young learners but experience shows that it is a matter about which they need guidance if their learning is to be effective. In following chapters there are some suggestions about various ways of learning vocabulary and, whatever strategies are used by teachers, they will be more effective if pupils are given reasons for learning. Suffice it here to say that if a 'learning vocabulary' homework is deemed suitable for a particular selection of words:

- the **need** for it should be made explicit (i.e. the pupils' need, in terms of the current **goal**);
- the exact **focus** of the learning should to be specified (are they learning for receptive use or productive use?);
- the **way to go about** the learning will be explained (see Chapter 10);
- the follow-up (a test or some other task) will reflect both the **objectives** and **the way they have learned.**

'How will we be tested on the learning homework?'

It seems to be axiomatic that what has been learned for homework must be tested. So pupils will have been taught to expect a test and it often simply takes the form of a series of words in English for the pupil to write the equivalents in the TL. It is worth remembering here that the test should accurately reflect what has been learned, so that the English into the TL test would only be valid when the goal of the unit involved **translation** (see **'What do you mean, LEARN?'** above).

'Why do we need a test?'

It might be argued with some justification that if the teacher does not test, the pupils will not do the task. However, it is also necessary to weigh up the value of the test and the time it takes against the time needed for other reinforcement activities which might be more important in the learning cycle.

When the above points have been debated, the teacher may still see the test as necessary in some circumstances. If that is the case, there are three other forms of testing which might be considered more appropriate, in reflecting the objective(s) of setting such homework, than the simple translation technique:

1   The teacher uses the same stimuli as in the initial presentation of the words (real objects, pictures, symbols or mime). The instruction is then to write the word in the TL.
2   The teacher presents the stimulus but the response is **oral** rather than written. This may be more appropriate than a written test, if the words are to be used for a spoken task, such as a tape-recording or video to be sent to a partnership school.
3   A cloze test in which the gaps are the words learned for homework. (The words are supplied or not, depending on the teacher's objectives.) This would be appropriate if written material (a letter or a report) was the goal of the unit.

NB: if a test on vocabulary learned for homework is considered important it will be a teaching tool and not for **assessment** purposes. Tests which are done for reinforcement of learning are not complete once they have been done. The object of the test of learning is not to find out who has done the work and who has not, but in order to reinforce new vocabulary. Immediate feedback and follow-up remedial work is essential if the test if to achieve anything.

CiLT

3.   The vocabulary notebook

 IS IT NECESSARY FOR STUDENTS TO KEEP A VOCABULARY NOTEBOOK?

Opinion is divided about the value of the vocabulary note-book and it is not the purpose of this section to be dogmatic on the subject. It is perhaps a matter which is best discussed at the departmental level and then left to the individual teacher to make a decision for each class. The following notes are offered as a framework for discussion.

PROS	CONS
The proven efficacy of **organised** learning. There is some evidence to suggest that memory is assisted by sorting words into lists, according to different parts of speech.	Particularly with children the time taken for keeping a vocabulary book has to be balanced against all the other important activities. (Will there still be time for independent reading and listening as well as working on the vocabulary books?)
Through the notebook pupils can be taught to think about the **function** of the word rather than just the **form,** or how it is spelt.	What they write must be **accurate** or they will be learning from a faulty model. So frequent checking and correcting is essential. Has the teacher enough time?
Vocabulary growth is somewhat slowed by 'forgetting'. Almost half the new words 'learned' seem to get lost.	Does keeping a vocabulary notebook create a 'word-for-word' mentality?
The vocabulary book serves as a focus for regular revision.	Does it create 'translation' thinking when we hope to encourage them to think in the language?

 IF A NOTEBOOK IS KEPT WHAT SHOULD GO INTO IT?

When the above matters have been considered, it may well be decided that for the more able language learners benefits could be gained from their keeping vocabulary note-books. In this case, it would be worthwhile planning in advance how pupils will be taught to compile and use them.

The simplest course of action is for the teacher to get the pupils to copy down whatever crops up. However, if the vocabulary to be included is what is already in the textbook there is little to be added by having them simply copy down the new words. It is perhaps better to to have the new vocabulary grouped according to:

CILT

- topics (within the Areas of Experience); or
- grammatical function (verbs, prepositions, nouns, adjectives, adverbs).

SIMPLE RULES FOR KEEPING THE NOTEBOOK

It is worthwhile spending a little time at the beginning of the year and at intervals throughout the course in teaching pupils how to organise their notebooks. Then they need to be given simple instructions about what goes into them.

- The quickest entry is the TL word and the English. However, this does have the drawback of being contrary to the spirit of TL teaching and can lead to a word-for-word translation mentality. A compromise which some teachers use is to have the English written in pencil, to be erased as soon as it is known, thus signalling that the English is just a prop for initial understanding.

- The TL word and a graphic (picture, symbol, icon). For younger learners this is the arrangement most consistent with TL teaching but it has the disadvantage that it takes pupils time to draw pictures and the drawings usually become more important than the words. Furthermore, it is not all meanings which can be represented in this way.

For more advanced learners, there are two other possible sorts of entry, which may be slower but more useful:

- the new word and a synonym (and/or antonym);
- the TL word with a meaningful definition.

Either of these latter systems of keeping a vocabulary notebook, or a combination of the two, can be linked to some work with mono-lingual dictionaries and/or a thesaurus. Time spent on such activities is an invaluable way of teaching learners to get beyond the initial 'meaning' of words (see Chapter 8).

What can be stated unequivocally is that when vocabulary notebooks **are** kept, the teacher will need to check that what goes into them is **accurate** and in accordance with **the rules** which he or she lays down, for instance:

- nouns must always appear with an article (or possessive adjective);

- nouns should be grouped together according to gender (colour-coding or the position of each gender on the page);

CiLT

- verbs should be accompanied by the appropriate tag (probably the infinitive, but maybe the relevant pronoun).

Pupils need to be encouraged to **use** their notebooks for revising the contents, for testing each other and to practise in new structures learned later.

4. Playing games: a waste of time?

'I don't like German because all you do is play games.'

'I liked French in the first two or three years — but when we started to . . .
. . . do grammar
or) . . . prepare for the GCSE
or) . . . just do writing)   *. . . I hated it.'*

These two apparently contradictory types of comment may be two sides of the same coin. There is certainly something to be said for playing games purely for fun, particularly in the early stages of introducing children to a new language. The proliferation of language clubs in primary schools in recent years and the sort of remarks quoted above bear witness to children's enjoyment of this aspect of language learning. However, to play games **just for fun** or to allow games to monopolise language learning in the classroom can be wasteful of valuable time. The second sort of remark above suggests that serious pupils can become irritated by what they see as pointless activities when all other pressures in their lives are telling them to work hard and 'get good results'.

What is needed is a more balanced approach to word-games throughout KS3 and KS4. It helps the more serious minded to accept the idea of playing games if they are 'let into the secret' about the contribution of a particular game to the goal of the moment. The pupils who just like playing games because it is easy and enjoyable can also benefit by being given reasons which go beyond immediate gratification. (The idea of 'letting the pupils into the secrets' is further developed in Chapter 10).

The field of English as a Foreign Language has provided us with a wealth of suggestions of games to play in teaching English and some of these have filtered into MFL teaching. What is not always made explicit is the extent to which these games contribute to a particular objective.

It is worthwhile looking at the commonest of the word-games to see how they can be used to fit what we know about ways of learning vocabulary.

CiLT

The following three principles are fundamental to whether or not we choose a particular word-game and more importantly, how we play it:

- words are best learned and practised in a context;
- the majority of words which we learn are not actually taught, but imbibed as a result of doing something else;
- there will only be a point to the game if the vocabulary content is chosen from words which are high-frequency words, used in the same way as they are in the game.

When the above principles are borne in mind as the reason for playing a particular game and attention is drawn to them, word-games can have a particular role to play in teaching vocabulary.

 ## VARIATIONS ON PELMANISM (played in pairs)

A series of pairs of cards are laid face down in random order. Players take it in turn to turn over two cards and keep the pair if they match.

1 Half the cards have the TL word and half the English word.

> When we are trying to get learners to think in the FL it is not easy to justify this variation in mainstream teaching. However, for those with special learning needs developing **Language Awareness** is one of the most important reasons for MFL learning. Pupils whose recognition of English word-forms is very elementary may therefore benefit from playing this variation of Pelmanism.

2 Half the cards have the TL word and half a picture or symbol.

> This works well for reinforcing simple **recognition** of the written form, if that is what is appropriate for the particular selection of words being used for the game.

3 All cards have picture pairs with no words, such as those for young English children, where the game involves **saying** the words (*zwei Hünder, dos perros, deux chiens*, etc).

> This is a useful game where the **goal** of the Unit of Work is something like: '*We are going to send a tape to our partnership class, telling them about . . .* ' This variation is a way of focusing on **speaking.** Of course, there needs to be a clear instruction about how to proceed and they do need to be monitored. Otherwise, they will play the game in English!

4   TL word and a common 'twin'. The content of the cards can be adapted for playing at any level from complete beginners to very advanced. Sets of words can be created using the following types of 'twinning':

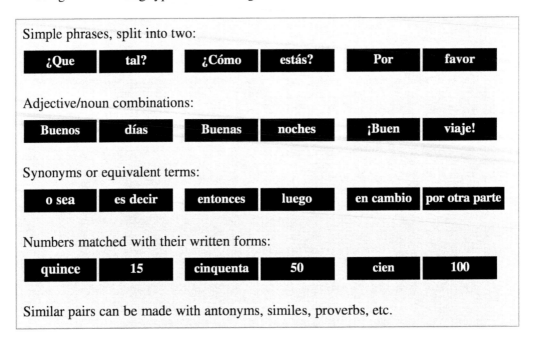

Simple phrases, split into two:

¿Que	tal?	¿Cómo	estás?	Por	favor

Adjective/noun combinations:

Buenos	días	Buenas	noches	¡Buen	viaje!

Synonyms or equivalent terms:

o sea	es decir	entonces	luego	en cambio	por otra parte

Numbers matched with their written forms:

quince	15	cinquenta	50	cien	100

Similar pairs can be made with antonyms, similes, proverbs, etc.

Playing a game of this sort for five minutes could be more valuable than sending the pupils away to 'learn the numbers' for homework. With numbers, the most important skills are listening and speaking and to a lesser degree reading. The ability to **spell** numbers is only needed, possibly, for letter-writing (numbers 1–10) and yet much time is often wasted on demanding that pupils learn how to do this.

An additional way of making the most of pelmanism is to have the cards made by the pupils for homework. Different groups in the class are given different topic areas for which to make sets of cards. They then 'play' the game with each other's sets in class. Getting them to **create the cards for themselves** is not only helpful in terms of saving the teacher's time, but it is also a way of getting pupils to think about which words go together and getting them to copy accurately!

BINGO/LOTTO (played as a whole class)

Played in its traditional form this is an excellent game for practising hearing and understanding numbers. It can easily be graded in difficulty to suit the level of the learner:

'On your blank grid write down any 9 numbers between 1 and 10' or *'any number between 30 and 60'* or *'Write down five numbers each including a 5 or each including a 4'*, etc. (Of course, the teacher may wish to use TL for these instructions.)

Bingo/Lotto can also be a useful way of practising those words which are more likely to be needed for the receptive skills than the productive skills. In this case, the words would be printed on the bingo grid instead of numbers.

NOUGHTS AND CROSSES (whole class team-game, played on the board)

Virtually any set of vocabulary can be practised and there can be incentives to make them think of **combinations of words** or **words in context** built into the rules, for example:

- Practising talking about the family: *'You must use mon/ma or mes to get a nought or a cross: mon père, ma mère, mes parents.'*
- Practising talking about school subjects: *'You must use a verb to get a nought or a cross: habla inglés, estudiamos matemáticas, Señor Jones enseña la historia'.*
- Practising prepositions: *'You must give a whole sentence, including the preposition to get a nought or a cross: Sie kommt aus Bremen. Die Bank ist gegenüber dem Supermarkt.'*

ANAGRAMS (in pairs or as a whole-class team-game, played on the board)

These are a well tried way of focusing on the spelling of new words. They should be words that they have already met and practised in the spoken form and they should be used in context **before** and **after** playing the game. There is little point in anagrams unless the words concerned are those which learners will need frequently for **writing** (see the consideration of what vocabulary should be taught in Chapter 1).

Asking the pupils to **write anagrams themselves** to try on their class-mates is an equally valuable activity, particularly if they are told that they will not have the words in front of them when they are checking the results!

WORD SEARCHES (individually or in pairs)

Because word searches are popular with children and because they keep them quiet they are often allowed to take more time than they are worth. However, getting the pupils to make up their **own** word searches to try out on each other is an excellent way of encouraging accurate copying for an obvious purpose. When the other pupils actually do these searches they should be instructed to write down the words they find, rather than just to put a line through them.

 ## CROSSWORDS (individually or in pairs)

These can be a very useful way of reinforcing vocabulary for the more able language learners. They are also popular with people of any age. They do have the advantage of making the learner think, particularly when the clues are also in the TL, and as is mentioned elsewhere getting pupils to give definitions of words is an excellent way of making them associate word and meaning. If the teacher has access to appropriately targeted crosswords, they will be a useful alternative in terms of discrimination.

NB: if the teacher has to compile them him- or herself, it is easier to produce the sort of crossword which does not have to fit into a square.

 ## I WENT TO MARKET, AND I BOUGHT SOME BANANAS . . .
(best played in groups, rather than with the whole class)

Each individual repeats the previous statement and adds an item of his own. The effort of memory creates an immediate purpose for the activity. There is an infinite number of ways in which this game can be adapted for practising vocabulary needed for **listening** and **speaking goals.** ('My grandmother went to the doctor's because she had earache, backache . . .', 'We went school and we took our pens, our pencils . . .', etc.)

 ## CRACKING CODES AND SOLVING PUZZLES (individually or in pairs)

There are commercially available books of codes to crack and puzzles to solve. They may have some entertainment value, if little else. However, getting pupils **to write their own codes** for their partners to crack, using recently encountered vocabulary, has the same advantage as composing anagrams. If pupils are in a computer club at school, or if they have their own computer at home, they can easily be persuaded into doing this sort of thing as an alternative to playing video games! (See Chapter 8.)

CiLT

5.   The old skills revisited

Effective vocabulary teaching is a question of:

*   introducing new words in **a context;**
*   gearing the context to **the needs** and **interests** of the learner;
*   creating opportunities for **frequent practice;**
*   making opportunities for learners to **encounter new words incidentally.**

Language teachers will have fairly strong views about what has contributed to their own proficiency in the language(s) they teach. Most people will feel they have benefited from and, indeed, sometimes enjoyed most of the following seven language learning activities:

*   extended listening;
*   translation from the target language;
*   translation into the target language (sometimes quaintly referred to as 'prose');
*   extended reading;
*   summarising;
*   dictation;
*   transcription.

Because all these things have played a part in their own language acquisition they may have mixed feelings about not including them in their teaching today, forbidden as they may appear to be by the 'new orthodoxy' or excluded, as it sometimes seems, by the time taken to fulfil the requirements of the National Curriculum. This may be a suitable point at which to re-consider to what extent any or all the above techniques can be beneficial in developing vocabulary in a meaningful way.

Changes in fashions in language teaching have meant that sometimes very important aspects of language provision have been forced out by changes in emphasis. The somewhat limited interpretation of Communicative Language Teaching, with its emphasis on spoken negotiation, has indeed improved learners' ability to be confident in getting what they want by **speaking.** What has been lost in the process is the development of the receptive skills, which many learners used to find easier to acquire!

LISTENING

USE OF THE TARGET LANGUAGE BY THE TEACHER

One of the threads running through the National Curriculum has been the importance of getting pupils to accept the foreign language as the normal means of communication in the classroom. In recent years, many language teachers have become proficient in achieving this. New vocabulary is usually introduced or explained by the techniques of using pictures (either carefully prepared or improvised on the spot) by using mime, by giving synonyms and antonyms, by definitions in the TL, etc. Many teachers are also aware of the difference between the written and the spoken language and may therefore choose to explain the meaning of a heard word by simply writing it on the board. This development in TL teaching is certainly one of the best ways in the classroom context of ensuring that frequently needed vocabulary is heard often enough to become fixed.

THE TARGET LANGUAGE AS A MEDIUM FOR LEARNING SOMETHING ELSE

The most effective way of encountering words incidentally is clearly through living for a period in one of the countries where the TL is spoken. However, as this is not an option for the majority of our learners, although the school visit abroad can be a valuable substitute[1]. Some people would say that from the point of view of vocabulary acquisition an equally useful strategy is to teach another subject in the target language, such as is commonly done in Canada and some international schools in Europe. There are certainly those who are planning to increase the amount of teaching of other subjects through the medium of the foreign language and it is something which can be done on a small scale from quite an early age, even within the ordinary classroom. If the subject matter is not entirely unfamiliar to the learners (elementary scientific experiments, easy sums, basic geography or history, for example) and is well supported by visuals, young learners can get a sense of achievement and confidence in understanding the foreign language at the same time as acquiring words by hearing them in context.

WIDENING THE CHOICE OF MATERIALS

The third way of ensuring that learners have the opportunity to enrich their vocabulary by **incidental encounter** is by the teachers providing learners with a variety of listening material in addition to what is needed for the initial presentation of selected new vocabulary. There is much excellent recorded listening material with the newer courses and the advantages of using this material for regular listening practice in the classroom are generally agreed. However, if it can be accepted that acquiring vocabulary is best done incidentally while doing something else (speaking with natives, listening and

---

1   The importance of giving pupils an opportunity for a visit abroad, as listed among the 40 'opportunities' in the N.C. programmes of study, is one which should be taken seriously by all schools. Such a visit does indeed contribute to vocabulary extension and language enhancement, although as is detailed in *Crossing frontiers* (Pathfinder 30) the main possibilities for such a visit will be in the field of cultural awareness.

reading) the teacher does need to provide opportunities at all levels for listening which goes beyond what is currently the norm.

In addition to commercial recordings, some teachers build up a stock of home-made materials which can be valuable resources for different levels of learners. What has been made by people known to the pupils, even if it may not be technically perfect, can have a greater impact on learners than course material, which is often presented like any other classroom exercise. (For teachers who have not yet tried creating their own listening materials there are some suggestions in Appendix C.)

- Listening in the classroom is not always just for testing, but it often looks like that to the learners. The teacher should, ideally, avoid saying:
  'Now we're going to do a listening comprehension' or
  'Here's a listening test'.
- Listening as a **teaching strategy** is more effective when this approach is used:
  'Now let's all listen to these (TL) people speaking about . . .'
- Pupils are more likely to make the effort if they see the teacher listening as well (and sometimes not quite hearing).
- The activity will be more productive in terms of vocabulary acquisition if they understand that the teacher is teaching them **how to listen**, rather than just judging them.

READING

It was during the period of the Schools' Council Projects in the 1970s when the best reading material was produced. There was a variety of texts (historical, fictional, cartoons, jokes, factual, and so on) and although they were written in simplified language they looked like books of their time and there was a selection of different styles, so that they did not look like school books. What would be useful would be for a publisher to look again at these books and to use them as a model for reproducing similar material in a more modern idiom and with lower linguistic demands upon the pupils. Meanwhile, there is a certain amount that can be done by individual departments in the following ways:

- creating class libraries with a wide variety of reading types;
- teaching pupils how to read (see Chapter 10);
- giving them time in class and for homework to use books;
- monitoring that they are doing the job, without letting testing become an objective in itself.

It is important to create in young learners the habits of developing their vocabulary learning habits through using a wider range of reading than is normally available to them at present. Probably the best way of doing this is to create small individual class libraries which will include any published material available and anything the teacher has been able to collect from other sources.

At the post-16 stage there are clearly many more possibilities of providing a wide range of reading materials. The excellent newspapers and tapes published by Authentik, a campus company of Trinity College Dublin, and available in several languages, are ideal from both points of view. There are various possible ways of using the press and radio extracts which are included but one of the best ways is to give students the whole paper and tape to study over a period of time (say, a holiday period) possibly with instructions to concentrate on certain items. This is then followed by a test written and aural, using the sorts of techniques suggested in the *feuille de travail* or testing types which are peculiar to the examination board. If this becomes a regular activity during an advanced course there is really no need for them to study lists of words out of context as sometimes happens at present.

TRANSLATION FROM THE TARGET LANGUAGE

The reason why translation became unfashionable was that it approached language learning from an angle which actually interfered with acquiring the skill of thinking in the language and if it was begun too early it encouraged the view that language was only real if it was our own language. Furthermore, it was a hard exercise which involved a lot of thinking and research in dictionaries. For the last reason and because the art of translation does demand precise analysis of words in context it is still irreplaceable as a skill to be practised at a high level of language study. For example, translation from the target language into English is an excellent activity for teachers themselves to continue practising to keep their own proficiency well honed.

As far as translating every word newly heard or read into English is concerned, the development of TL teaching has shown that this is simply not necessary and interferes with the direct association of meaning with words. However, teachers will still make the judgement that sometimes a translation into English is the quickest way of explaining a new word. This is not something they should feel guilty about, but they should make a point of supporting the translation with one of the other techniques for presentation and should put the word into a context as quickly as possible. Then the initial use of the English as a prop will only be needed once.

At the post-16 stage a little free translation to be undertaken as an occasional exercise is a valuable way of getting learners to think about precise meanings of words in particular contexts. However, to have all new texts translated into English, *'just to be sure they really understand them'* is ill-advised, encouraging a translation view of language which runs counter to the main aim of helping learners to think **in the language**.

TRANSLATION INTO THE TARGET LANGUAGE

At a level somewhere beyond 'A' level, translating into the target language can be a valuable exercise in developing precise understanding of both languages. For beginners and intermediate learners there would appear to be no justification for learners to translate from their mother tongue. Even if the **goal** of the moment is to speak or write about an aspect of their own lives (in a communication with their correspondents) the preparation is best done by their writing a few notes **in the target language**, rather than preparing in English first.

SUMMARISING

This is one of the best approaches to the reinforcement of vocabulary — and it does not have to be left for more advanced learners. It can be done as soon as pupils are able to understand and use the third person of the commonest verbs in the past.

- The teacher speaks to the class as a whole, along these lines:
  either *'At the weekend . . .* (or *Yesterday evening . . .* or *During the holidays . . .) I went to . . . and . . .';*
  or recounts a previously known story, maybe illustrating it with sketches or mime at the same time (*Hansel and Gretel* goes down well with thirteen and fourteen year olds, if the gruesome side is emphasised!);
  or (at KS4) recounts a real story from the news.
- The pupils are asked to note key-words (or the teacher may choose to identify them, writing them on the board as he or she speaks).
- The pupils then have to re-tell the story (to the whole class or in pairs — see Appendix B) using their own words.

The same technique can be used for reinforcing new vocabulary using a written text. Instead of jotting down key-words, learners can be asked to find a suitable title, or a series of headings, to use as the basis for producing a summary in their own words.

DICTATION

When the emphasis in language learning was on written accuracy, the formal dictation used to play a prominent part in developing that accuracy. With the advent of a more communicatively based approach, it was realised that the time taken to achieve competence in this purely academic skill was out of all proportion to its usefulness in terms of real language usage.

However, there are occasions when reasonable written accuracy is what is needed to achieve a particular **goal.** There is little point in having pupils making wall displays or writing to correspondents if what they write is not accurate. To say that they can get an A* in the GCSE without being completely accurate is irrelevant in terms of the professed aims and objectives of teaching languages!

It is, then, in the field of written accuracy that the dictation of individual words or phrases can be a useful way of practising new vocabulary, providing always that the vocabulary has been identified as necessary for **written expression.**

Dictation can also be a helpful teaching device to practise the changes in sub-elements of vocabulary (verb endings, case endings, silent letters, etc.)

TRANSCRIPTION

This is a development of the traditional dictation and one which is worth mentioning at this stage. Although the transcription is probably inappropriate for pre-16 learners, it is a most successful exercise for more advanced students as well as for teachers wishing to hone their own language skills in a second language. Transcription differs from dictation in that the stimulus consists of the recording of a passage of real spoken language, as opposed to the teacher's slow reading, as in a dictation. The student can listen as often as necessary and may even use a dictionary to assist him or her in the task.

Apart from its intrinsic use in extending and reinforcing vocabulary, this is also a skill which teachers of advanced students find particularly useful in creating a written version of a piece of listening material, for further exploitation and study.

For this purpose, recordings from sound radio are generally superior to video recordings where the pictures tend to interfere with concentration. (See Appendix A for the best source of radio broadcasts available in this country.)

6.   Verbs are words too

Whether we consider verbs as an element in the grammatical structure of a language or whether we look upon them as items of vocabulary is not a matter which needs to be debated here. However, a consideration of the ways of teaching and learning verbs does fit neatly into the present volume. The practical difference between learning, say, a noun and a verb lies in the multiplicity of different forms that the verb has in the commonly taught languages. It is this considerable body of words and 'sub-words' which can cause such confusion and despair among learners.

In traditional grammar-translation teaching, verbs were taught as though they had a life of their own. Verbs were introduced in strict rotation: present tense (regular, irregular, interrogative, imperative, negative interrogative, negative imperatives) future tenses, past tenses, and so on. And all these forms were given names and learned in a particular order (first person singular, second person singular . . .) The tidy mind of the grammatically motivated teacher had no bounds. Even long since obsolete forms were taught to all learners because they completed the jig-saw and somehow the job did not seem complete without them. The result of this approach was a very thorough understanding of verbs by the most able language learners but it was also the source of complete confusion for the vast majority and it certainly did not lead to the oral fluency of any of them.

Communicative Language Teaching has led some teachers to take the completely opposite line in teaching verbs: in the most extreme cases, verbs are taught as items of vocabulary like any other parts of speech, whenever they occur, or when the need arises to fulfil a particular task. This approach ignores the tremendous potential of drawing attention to the patterns which exist and using these patterns as an aid to learning with understanding.

The compromise position adopted by many teachers is as follows:

- teach new verb forms from the point of view of the need of the moment (which verbs or parts of verbs you will need in order to achieve the current **goal**);
- define the words as they crop up in the course of reading or listening (or, in an ideal world, as they are being used to teach another subject);
- at an appropriate stage, take a group of parts of the verb and draw attention to the pattern with other verbs (formation, regularities, irregularities);
- practise the new verbs/ parts of verbs in **drills and** in a **realistic context;**

- set tasks which involve using them orally and possibly in writing , in ways which are realistic and will aid recall;
- continue drilling and using verbs in context at frequent intervals and with different topic areas;
- avoid using grammatical labels until an advanced stage (say, post-16).

As an introduction to the imperfect tense, for example, pupils might hear people talking about life in the past or see some writing about what things used to be like.

Then the following goal could be specified:

'We're going to ask some senior citizens what life was like when they were young, then we're going to tell our partners in (TL country) what we have found out. Their teachers are going to organise the same sort of report and then we'll compare life here with life there.'

The next step will be to go to the text which was initially read or heard fairly superficially for interest or information. This time the tense in question will be examined and rules for formation specified. Some practice will naturally follow.

This sequence may be sufficient for the learners to tackle the particular task in hand, but if the new tense is to become part of their permanent language *baggage* it will need to be **over-learned.**

It is at this stage that **drilling** will be most useful. Apart from those who have learned a second language by total immersion, most proficient foreign language speakers will confess to the need for **verb practice** or **drilling.**

Drilling need not necessarily be a chore for learners, but if they are actually to enjoy the experience it needs to be kept to **very frequent short bursts** and presented in terms they can appreciate:

- the professional sportsman needs to continue to practise the basic skills long after becoming proficient at his sport;
- people go jogging or do aerobics to keep in trim;
- actors exercise in the gym and need to practise their lines long after they think they know them;
- musicians practise their scales even when they are expert concert performers;
- **speakers of foreign languages need to keep practising their verbs.**

CiLT

Drills are successful if they are done at high-speed with a whole class by the teacher, but there are additional advantages if learners are trained to work in pairs (see Appendix B). The sort of verb drills which are most useful are those which spring from actual speech patterns:

1 *Aimes-tu . . ? Oui, j'aime . . . Non, je n'aime pas . . .*
   Aimes-tu les escargots? Oui, j'aime les escargots. Non, je n'aime pas les escargots.
2 *Tomber. Je . . ? Il . . ?* (followed, on different occasions, by other common regular *-er* verbs, followed by *-ir* verbs, followed by irregulars, etc).
3 As for 2 but using the English for the stimulus.

It is important to remember that the drill is only a half-way stage in the learning process. Immediately after practising a verb in this way, opportunities should be given to practise in a realistic context.

NB: the ability to chant a paradigm '*ich bin, du bist, er/sie/es . . .*' is not very useful. Learning a list of infinitives, before the use of the infinitive is understood or needed and before the learners can use more frequently occurring parts of the verb, will not lead to the automatic production which we are seeking.

7. Techniques worth exploring

 ## TOTAL PHYSICAL RESPONSE

This is a technique whereby new words are presented with physical actions to be copied by the learners. Many people have found this a useful aid to memorising words and ensuring that they are remain linked to their meanings. It is most appropriate for learning action verbs and in its simplest form it involves pupils obeying commands: 'Come in. Sit down. Go to the board. Write . . . Look . . . Listen . . .', etc.

Some teachers take the technique much further by doing regular exercise of verbs based on aerobics, using a musical background and combining verbs with other parts of speech: 'touch your knees', 'raise your arms', 'knock on the door', etc.

The idea can be further developed by adding actions to everything that is said. For example, a simple dialogue involving booking into a hotel may go like this:

Teacher:	*Bonjour, monsieur*	(teacher bows)
Pupils:	*Bonjour, madame*	(pupils bow)
Teacher:	*Vous désirez?*	(teacher draws a question mark in the air)
Pupils:	*Avez-vous une chambre, s'il vous plaît?*	(pupils hold up one finger, then put heads on hands as for sleeping)
Teacher:	*Pour combien de personnes?*	(draws a question-mark in the air)
Pupils:	*Pour trois personnes*	(raise three fingers)
Teacher:	*Pour combien de nuits?*	(a rough sketch of a moon on the board and a question-mark)
Pupils:	*Pour trois nuits*	(three fingers and point at the moon)
Teacher:	*Avec douche ou salle de bain?*	(pulls imaginary cord to indicate 'douche' and turns on the taps of the bath)
Pupils:		(copy whatever action is appropriate for the response)

When the dialogue has been practised as above, the class splits into pairs and practises in the same way. The next stage is to give each of the speakers a 'character' (a bad-tempered old hotel manager and bossy customer, perhaps). The writer has observed this sort of teaching with large classes of Year 10 boys who had been taught to take the matter quite seriously and clearly benefited from associating words with physical representations of them.

CiLT

DRAWING TIME

Some learners find it helpful to imagine time visually. The teacher may either point to his or her position in the room or draw on the board, to represent tenses:

This is sometimes further refined with squiggly lines for the imperfect and dots for the past definite, etc. Whenever adverbs of time are mentioned they are accompanied by pointing or drawing, according to the above sketch.

LINKING WORDS

Another way of learning new words is to make a deliberate link between the TL word and an English word which sounds or looks similar. This is a memory aid which has been supported by some serious research and with which a lot of learners feel comfortable. The system works best with concrete nouns and works like this:

The Spanish word for CAT is GATO
Imagine a CAT eating a lovely GATEAU

The Spanish for BEACH is PLAYA
Imagine you PLAY A game on the beach

The Spanish for DOOR is PUERTA
Imagine a hotel PORTER opening the door for you   *These examples are quoted from Gruneberg's Linkword series*

The learners are asked to hold the pictures in their mind's eye for ten seconds before moving to the next word.

THE POSSIBILITIES OF PROVERBS

In KS4 and above, useful way of putting words into a memorable context is by learning proverbs or advertising jingles. Proverbs can be learned by pupils doing this sort of activity:

* matching up TL proverbs with their English equivalents;
* matching up TL proverbs with brief statements meaning the same;

- defining proverbs in their own words;
- telling (or writing) a story which illustrates the proverb.

THE WRITING ON THE WALL

What is on the wall can just be like wallpaper: it might brighten up the place but nobody ever looks at it. However, not only can it be beneficial to the pupils who prepare it, but it can also be used for vocabulary learning if the teacher remembers it is there! The following are some of the words on walls which have been seen on recent visits to schools and are pertinent to vocabulary acquisition:

- numbers 1–100. (The written forms of numbers do sometimes need to be **recognised**, although they are not often needed for **reproduction**);
- days of the week and/or months of the year (a board with cut-outs into which pupils insert the day, the date and the month, at the beginning of each lesson);
- cut-outs of animals hanging from a beam (labelled in the TL);
- a washing-line hanging from a beam with cut-out articles of clothing (labelled);
- all the question forms in the TL;
- classroom 'survival' phrases which pupils always have to use;
- illustrated subjects from the time-table (symbols they have invented);
- '*Nos amis français*' — photographs of an exchange visit to the school with pictures of pen-friends and their families and places they have visited, etc, all labelled in the TL;
- '*Notre petit-déjeuner français*' — obviously the day they put table-cloths on the school desks and brought in the coffee and croissants!
- '*On recherche . . .*' (Rogues gallery with descriptions in TL of the wanted criminals. Sometimes seen in DTP form);
- Coloured squares/balloons, etc with labels (handy to have on the wall whenever colours are needed);
- a blown-up map of the town, with symbols and labels in TL;
- a map of the relevant country, so that towns and region can be referred to when contexts are needed for new words.

8. Words and new technology

Effective vocabulary teaching is a question of:

- introducing new words in **a context;**
- gearing the context to **the needs** and **interests** of the learner;
- creating opportunities for **frequent practice;**
- making opportunities for learners to **encounter new words incidentally.**

Bearing this in mind it is worthwhile considering the value of new technologies in facilitating language acquisition.

VIDEO CAMERAS

The value of the camera (used sparingly) as a stimulus to learning vocabulary cannot be over-estimated. Great emphasis has been placed in this book on the importance of establishing appropriate **goals** for learners. It is highly desirable for these goals to be linked to real situations, which mainly depend on links with partners abroad (school, class, personal) but it is recognised that links take time to create and sometimes break in spite of people's best efforts. It is here that the video camera can be a good second best. For young learners it will probably be sufficient to say that the goal at the end of a Unit of Work will be to make a five minute video. (For example, learning the vocabulary for clothes can have as its goal a video of a mannequin parade. Learning food vocabulary can be given impetus by creating a series of advertisements for food as the goal.)

COMPUTERS

1   The most useful software on the computer from the point of view of language learning in general is still the **word processor**. The uses to which the word processor can be put have been detailed in various publications produced by the British Educational Communications and Technology Agency (BECTA, formerly NCET) (see Further reading). What is worth reiterating here is that the importance of accuracy when the **written word** is being used can be given more point when a professional piece of work for display is the immediate goal. If there is a TL spellchecker available as well the task becomes even more focused.

2 For pupils with their own computers, or post-16 students, an alternative (or addition) to keeping a vocabulary notebook is creating a personalised dictionary from the spelling section of the word processor. The value of sorting words into parts of speech has already been highlighted and the **custom dictionary** is an economical and efficient tool for doing this.

3 For older students a **dictionary/thesaurus** in the target language on the computer is an invaluable addition to the more conventional reference works.

4 This is not the place to advertise the vast range of **CD-ROMs and databases** which have been designed specifically for language learning. All that need be said is that they can be a useful resource for giving learners the opportunity to encounter new words in a meaningful context. It is also worth considering what is available to young learners in the TL countries such as electronic encyclopædias (for example, at the time of writing, a version of Encarta in the languages mentioned in this book has just been introduced).

5 The sorts of word-games outlined in Chapter 4 as well as more sophisticated versions of the same things are available in an electronic form for use on the computer. *Fun With Texts, Storyboard, Developing Tray,* etc are often popular with young learners but the provisos already mentioned should be borne in mind before long hours are spent on getting pupils to learn the spellings of words which will be infrequently used. If the texts created by the teacher include words such as interrogatives, common verbs, prepositions, conjunctions (which might be termed **key-words for multi-purpose use**) these **text manipulation packages** can be a great help.

6 In Chapter 4 (Playing games: a waste of time?) the value of getting pupils to make up their own word games was mentioned. On the page opposite is an example of the sort of activity children enjoy if they have access to a computer.

Pupil instructions

When you have cracked the code, you can take some new words you have learned recently and convert them into a similar code. Make sure you don't make any spelling mistakes! You can then try them out on your friends.

If you have a computer, you might find that one of the fonts supplied on the word processor will supply the symbols for you. For instance the code opposite was made with the font called **ZapfDingbats.**

A homework task

Here is the key. Can you work out the codes below?

In English

En español

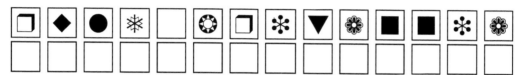

En français

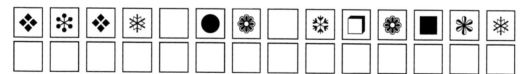

Auf Deutsch

THE INTERNET

This is an area which may not have an obvious link with acquiring vocabulary. However, when the points heading this chapter are remembered it will be seen that the World Wide Web is a potentially rich source of up-to-date reading material. As was pointed out under the heading of **Reading** (p23) the classrooms of today have become impoverished in this respect and where schools are already linked to the Internet a collection of suitable reading material can be downloaded for the purpose of creating a class 'library'. This will certainly take a certain amount of time on the part of the teacher but in schools with post-16 learners there is a dual benefit to be gained from these students surfing the Net on the teacher's behalf. They will need to be directed to appropriate sites by the teacher in the first place but selecting suitable material to be downloaded for use with younger pupils means that they themselves have to read it, and that is a way of improving their own vocabulary.

The other potential of the Internet which is being used by some schools is for e-mail exchange of letters with partner schools in the target country. This is probably the most effective way of providing opportunities for frequent encounter of new vocabulary in an authentic context.

Behind the scenes, the teachers in both schools will need to supply suggestions for material which would be useful to their pupils. Topics which are to be studied in any particular term can then form the basis for e-mail letters (see Townshend K, *E-mail* (CILT, 1997)). The mechanics of surfing the Net are dealt with in Atkinson T, *WWW/ the Internet* (CILT, 1998). Teachers of languages might well begin by using suitable search engines, such as Yahoo(fr) or Yahoo(de).

SATELLITE

TV PROGRAMMES

The skills of listening and reading have already been identified as areas which it is vital for learners to develop if they are to increase their vocabulary acquisition. In addition to providing a library of reading and listening materials from traditional sources and from the Web, the teacher now has access to the whole world of authentic television programmes.

Total language immersion may be possible only in the TL country, but the availability of programmes by satellite can be a valuable substitute and, if well directed by the teacher, may even be better than total immersion which can cause drowning! It is clearly not useful for a publication such as this to name particular programmes because of the ephemeral nature of television. However, it may be useful to suggest a few areas where teachers may find appropriate material.

For older learners there is clearly the whole gamut of news, documentaries and entertainment. For younger learners the selection is more difficult because it is important not to swamp them. A recent search of what is currently available has produced the following types of programme which could well be used with younger learners:

- science education programmes designed for much younger children in France, Spain or Germany. The fact that our Key Stage 3 and 4 learners will be vaguely familiar with the experiments, along with visual support in the form of simple graphics, should aid comprehension;
- games programmes, where young people are quick to understand what is happening, even when there is not complete comprehension of the spoken word;
- animal and wild-life programmes with strong visual appeal;
- exploration and travel documentaries.

Using short TV programmes such as these can give pupils a sense of achievement: they may find that they can understand what is happening, even when the language is quite difficult. Giving learners the opportunity to hear genuine speech for purposes which are not patently didactic is a very important side of vocabulary acquisition.

The TEXT facility

Most television channels have a text facility which could be an ideal **reading resource**. There are areas here which the teacher could use for whole-class teaching or where individuals or small groups could be given specific reading tasks. The most obvious place to find this material is in the interest areas which are dearest to the hearts of the young person:

- the world of popular music. (On some foreign language channels, there is information about groups, concerts, recordings, charts, etc.);
- the world of sport. (Fixtures, league-tables, information about teams and players, etc.)

In addition to these two areas of interest, Televisión Español has under **Guía Joven** various sections which could be of interest and intelligible to younger learners:

- *Turismo/Viajes:* a series of information pages describing certain towns and regions;
- *Discos:* discos más vendidos;
- *Pasatiempos;*
- *Juegos ('Mensajes ocultos').*

Another interesting section which should be accessible to quite elementary learners of Spanish is the topic of *Informática* itself. When discussing Information Technology, the key words are in English and furthermore, pupils will generally be vaguely familiar with the content of these pages. An ability to understand authentic language such as the following (and indeed the texts of which these are the headings) could be a valuable way of building confidence:

'El error de los Pentium'

'Estados Unidos busca nuevas leyes para regular los daños procudidos por el uso de teclados y pantallas de ordenador . . .'

Introducción a Internet:

- Origen — desarrollo — internet en el mundo — ventajas y utilidad
- ¿Qué necesita para . . ?
- A través de la voz . . .
- Diccionario interno

'Las tarjetas inteligentes: los usuarios cargarón sus tarjetas-chip 27.000 millones de veces en un año . . .'

In German, the following TEXT pages are worthy of exploration:

- on the Eurosport Deutsch channel: News, Fussball, TV heute;
- Vida Zwei (the TV channel is mainly music videos) but the text has news about the charts, concerts, etc;
- Viva (a general entertainment channel) has TEXT pages on: City News Berlin, Touren, Sport', etc.

There is a genuine motivation to find out about these things and to compare information gleaned in this way with what they already know. The teacher's only problem may be to ensure that pupils keep in proportion the time spent on browsing the text!

The TEXT facility can also be used for more specific vocabulary practice. Take, for example the departure and arrival times from Frankfurt airport. At the time of writing, these are available in French (TV5) or in German (Euronews).

Authentic material such as this can be used effectively to reinforce new vocabulary through repetitive questioning:

CiLT

En français	Auf Deutsch
Départs A quelle heure part l'avion pour Londres? Il part à 9 heures 25. C'est bien 9 heures 25 du matin? Ah non, c'est 9 heures 25 du soir. Il est à l'heure? Non, il a quinze minutes de retard.	**Abfahrt** Wann fliegt die Maschine nach London? Sie fliegt um 9.25 Uhr. Ist das um 9.25 morgens? Nein, das ist 9.25 abends. Landet sie pünklich? Nein, sie hat 15 Minuten Verspätung.
Arrivées A quelle heure arrive l'avion de Paris? Il arrive à 20 heures 15. Il est à l'heure? Non, il a une demi-heure de retard.	**Ankunft** Wann landet die Maschine nach Amsterdam? Sie landet um 20.15 Uhr. Sie hat eine halbe Stunde Verspätung.
Also to practise the **future:** A quelle heure va partir . . . va arriver . . ? A quelle heure partira . . ? . . . arrivera . . ?	

SUBTITLES

Satellite TV offers another opportunity for learning vocabulary through absorption in the form of **subtitles.** There are two sorts of titles available from time to time:

- English or American films with TL subtitles;
- TL films or documentaries with subtitles in the TL (designed initially for deaf viewers);

Each of these facilities can be an invaluable way of absorbing new vocabulary at an intermediate to advanced level, although language learners do need a certain amount of training in disciplining themselves to read and listen at the same time.

RADIO

While on the subject of the potential value of satellite, it should not be forgotten that radio programmes are also available by satellite and for advanced learners (and teachers wishing to keep up with what is happening in the world beyond the UK) the radio has always been an excellent source of information.

Depending on the area of the UK, the sound from long- or short-wave broadcasts can be poor to non-existent. The sound from satellite broadcasts is perfect and there is a far wider choice than on conventional radio.

9.   Focus on . . .

Particularly for the abler learners, though not exclusively the most advanced, it is a worthwhile exercise get pupils to reflect occasionally on the reasons they all have to study a language within the National Curriculum. In this way, they may come to understand that communicative competence for some imaginary future use is not the only, or even the most significant reason for this requirement. There will be occasions in teaching a language (a whole lesson or a part of a lesson) when teachers will wish to focus specifically on some aspect of vocabulary for its own sake, without gearing it to any particular communicative objective. In this chapter we will consider some of the possibilities.

LANGUAGE AWARENESS

It is not long ago that what was being advocated by some people was a general programme of Language Awareness before pupils embarked upon a particular Foreign Language. The writers of the National Curriculum have decided that that is not the way forward. Although Language Awareness is mentioned as one of the aims of language teaching, we have now reached the situation when the aim of heightening pupils' awareness of language has been minimised in most classrooms.

It can be a useful exercise for teachers to consult with their English language colleagues about areas where language awareness can best be raised in the MFL classroom.

To deal with the following issues **in English** will mean that pupils can more easily make connections with their own language and see the ways in which vocabulary expands in roughly the same way in all languages. It is suggested that in each case the starting point should be the English word, demonstrating the particular phenomenon of derivations. From here it is a natural step to move on to derivations of a similar sort in the TL.

CiLT

Where do words come from?

New words for new worlds: coining

English		Français	
mini-skirt	track-suit	la navette	un baladeur
trainers	shell-suit	une croissanterie	une jardinerie
telephone	television	une grillerie	une droguerie
micro-chip	mouse	un aéroglisseur	les puces
hardware	software	les bébés éprouvettes	une souris
test-tube babies	pacemakers	le must	le look
compact discs	body-building	un video-clip	un spot publicitaire
		les stimulateurs-cardiaques	

New words for new worlds: borrowing

English	Español	Français	Deutsch
From French:	**From English:**	**From English:**	**From English:**
Restaurant	El coca-cola light	Le camping	der Computer
Menu Soup	El waterpolo	Le caravaning	der Jogging
Salmon	Un hooligan	Le shampooing	die Hardware
Beef	La jet-set	Le parking Le smoking	die Software
Mutton		Un snack/Un self	die CD
Pork	**From Arabic:**	Une hi-fi	die Cassette
Architecture	Una almohada	Un talkie-walkie	die Stereo
Government	Un azulejo	Un walkman	die Hifi
Justice	El azafrán	Le far-west	die Rock Musik
Administration		Le body-building	die Maschine
Art Science		Un docker Le cake	das Internet
Cassette Disco			das Keyboard
		From other languages:	die Jeans
		Un toréador Un fjord	der Manager
		Une geisha Une guerilla	der Boss
		Un cappucino	das Business

New words for new worlds: proper names*

English	Español	Français	Deutsch
Hoover	un minipimer	Une poubelle	ein Tempo
Kleenex	(hand mixer)	Une guillotine	Selter
Sandwich	un suizo	L'eau de Javel	Hansaplast
to send someone	(teacake)	Une montgolfière	Frankfurter
to Coventry	el delco	Un judas	Berliner
	(distributor)	Une colonne Morris	der Kaba
	el cárter	Un apollon	ein Judas
	(crank-case)	Le champagne	
	una verónica	(from La Champagne)	
	(bull-fighting pass)	Le bordeaux	
		Un Perrier	
		Limoger quelqu'un	

* people and places

Words with a curiosity value

The vocabulary of slang can be an interesting topic for an occasional lesson at any stage beyond complete beginners. The following lists might serve as starters:

Slang and 'lazy words'

English	Español	Français	Deutsch
Let the pupils provide their own ideas but include: *Thingy* *Thingummy* *Whatsits*	hacer el canguro (to baby-sit) hacer el tonto (to act the fool) somos todos oídos (we're all ears) ir por su aire (to do one's own thing) *Un chisme*	Chouette Extra Terrible Génial Les petits coins T'as pigé? Le toubib T'es dingue, toi! Un mec Mon frangin Ma frangine Une patate Le resto Métro, boulot, dodo *Un truc . . .* *Un machin . . . Un bidule*	joggen, joben gemanaged Was geht? Er hat nicht alle Tassen im Schrank abgespaced einsame Spike klasse, genial die Kohle, verknallt schrill pennen *dingsda* *dingsbums, dasda*

THE SOUND OF WORDS

It is sometimes worthwhile spending a little time on the **sound** of words. There are four main reasons for doing this:

- most learners enjoy singing or speaking aloud, so long as they are not alone;
- natural shyness (particularly in the middle years of mixed gender classes) can be overcome by speaking together with others;
- concentrating on perfect copying of a native speaker helps the learner to realise that that the speech organs have to move differently in each language;
- the 'feel' of making foreign sounds becomes familiar to the learner.

SONGS

The first type of sound practice is the song. This is an area which has been covered comprehensively in Steven Fawkes's Pathfinder 25 (*With a song in my scheme of work*). It is sufficient here to emphasise how useful a specially constructed song can be in the context of vocabulary learning. It gives the teacher the opportunity for:

- frequent swift repetition in an enjoyable way;
- if gestures can be included, the element of total physical response can aid fixing the vocabulary.

CiLT

THE PRONUNCIATION LIST

In any language a pronunciation list is occasionally useful for the four reasons mentioned above. In French particularly, the pronunciation list has the additional purpose of drawing attention to the various possible **spellings** of different sounds. The example which appears here has been used at intermediate to advanced levels, but simpler lists can be constructed to meet the needs of different levels.

Liste de prononciation

OI	Les villag**eois** dans le b**ois** mangent des p**ois** avec les d**oigts**
	Il y avait une f**ois** un marchand de f**oie** qui vendait son f**oie** dans la ville de F**oie**
OU	Le voy**ou** à gen**oux** dans le tr**ou** plein de caill**oux** mange des ch**oux**
EUR	Le chauff**eur** de l'ambassad**eur** chante de tout c**œur** en graissant le mot**eur**
AIN IN	Le médec**in** prend le tr**ain** d'Ami**ens** après-dem**ain** pour aller à Berl**in**
U N	Chac**un** veut un empr**unt** au moment opport**un**. C'est comm**un**!
U	L'instit**ut** ten**u** par Monsieur Cam**us** est très conn**u**
OIN	J'ai bes**oin** d'un tém**oin** de l'accident du rond-p**oint**
È AIS	Je f**ais** expr**ès** d'avoir des fr**ais** au mois de m**ai**
É	L'employ**é** dévou**é** sera r**é**compens**é**
AN EN	Les cli**ents** du march**and** de g**ants** sont exig**eants**
EUIL	Du s**euil**, je vois mon portef**euille** dans le faut**euil**
EILLE	Je surv**eille** les ab**eilles** qui s'**éveillent** dans la corb**eille**
AIL	Les dét**ails** du b**ail** donnent du trav**ail**
AME	Les télég**rammes** pour mad**ame** viennent const**amme**nt d'une sage-f**emme**
OIR	Si j'ai bonne mém**oire**, l'arm**oire** provis**oire** est dans le laborat**oire** près du mir**oir**
A	J'ai marqué le result**at** de mes ach**ats** dans mon agend**a**. Ils sont adéq**uats**
OUR	Tous les j**ours** au carref**our** du faub**ourg**, le s**ourd** fait des disc**ours**
UI	Les fr**uits** c**uits** sont grat**uits** aujourd'**hui**
ONNE	La patr**onne** a téléph**oné**. Il n'y a pers**onne**? Ça m'ét**onne**!
ON OM	Les n**oms** et prén**oms** de mes compagn**ons** sont l**ongs**
EU	Les y**eux** de mon nev**eu** sont pleins de f**eu**
AU O EAU	Les **os** de mon d**os** sont en morc**eaux**
EU AU EAU	Les chev**eux** et les chev**aux** de mon nev**eu** sont b**eaux**
	Mon premier nev**eu** habite à Fontainebl**eau**
	Mon deuxième nev**eu** habite à Montr**eux**

TONGUE-TWISTERS

A third way of concentrating on the sound of words is by the use of the tongue-twister. Sometimes, this may be a way of tackling a particular sound which learners are finding difficult. At other times, a tongue twister may simply serve as a good warm-up device for the beginning of the lesson. Most of the examples here are not original, but it may be helpful to bring them together under the umbrella of vocabulary learning.

Mon oncle Léon ronfle longtemps dans sa chaise longue

Mon frère, Gaston, tombe souvent et rompt les boutons de son bon veston

Mon chat, Pompon, monte sur le rayon
où nous gardons la confiture de melon, les oignons et les concombres

Avez-vous vu la lune au-dessus des dunes?

Ce chat chauve caché sous six souches de sauge sèche

Si six scies scient six saucissons,
six cent six scies scient six cent six saucissons

Tonton, ton thé t'a-t-il ôté ta toux?

Toto le titi voit le tutu chez tata

Je pense que je peux — je pense que je peux — je pense que je peux . . .

Ma bague — ma bague — Ma bague — ma bague — Ma bague . . .

Panier — piano — panier — piano — panier — piano . . .

Un chasseur sachant sacher sans son chien
doit savoir chasser sans son chien

Les chaussettes de l'archiduchesse,
sont-elles sèches ou archi-sèches?

Dis donc, Zoë, tu sais qu'il y a eu soixante-cinq concerts
super-chers à Buenos-Aires, dont six au laser?

Des phrases à déchirer la mâchoire

Es spricht die Frau von Rubinstein:
Mein Hund, der ist nicht stubenrein
Blaukraut bleibt Blaukraut und Brautkleid
bleibt Brautkleid

Der Potsdamer Postkutscher putzt den
Potsdamer Postkutschwagen

Die böse Baronin von Fleetchen schikanierte
das Gretchen, ihr Mädchen,
bis ein schöner Prinz kam und Gretchen zur
Frau nahm.
Jetzt putzt Frau von Fleetchen bei Gretchen.

Kleine Kinder können keine Kirschkerne
knacken

Klemens Klasse kitzelt Klaras kleines Kind

Tausend Tropfen tröpfeln traurig, traurig
tröpfeln tausend Tropfen. Tip, tip, tup!

Trink keinen Rum, denn Rum macht dumm

Viele Fliegen fliegen vielen Fliegen nach

Zehn Zähne zieht mir der Zahnarzt
im Dezember

Wir Wiener Waschweiber würden weiße
Wäsche waschen,
wenn wir warmes, weiches Wasser hätten

Zehn Ziegen zogen zehn Zentner Zucker
zum Zoo

In Ulm, um Ulm und um Ulm herum

Zungenbrecher

CILT

Trabalenguas

El cielo está enladrillado. ¿Quién lo desenladrillará?
El desenladrillador que lo desenladrille, buen desenladrillador será
El perro de San Roque no tiene rabo, ¿por qué?
Porque Ramón se lo ha robado
Un triste tigre comía trigo en un trigal
Dos tristes tigres comían trigo en un trigal
Tres tristes tigres comían trigo en un trigal
Balbina vive en Valencia, Viviano vive en Bilbao
Daniel desayuna cada día. ¿Verdad?
El jamón que vende Gerónimo en el bar Gijón es famoso en Gerona
Once cervezas y doce zumos de naranja. Gracias.
¿Más más que menos o más menos que más?

INTONATION PRACTICE

Words which even quite young learners can appreciate are those which bear no meaning, but are extremely common in normal native speech. Occasionally, the teacher may wish to concentrate on those typical phrases used by native speakers which bear no 'meaning' but which express:

- hesitation;
- being unable to find the right word;
- strong **feelings.**

A little choral imitation practice, with special attention being paid to **intonation** is a good way of shaking off inhibitions about speaking which adolescents sometimes develop. If recordings of this sort of thing can be found, they can be most useful. Alternatively, it requires some acting ability on the part of the teacher:

English	Español	Français	Deutsch
. . . Ummm . . .	estee . . .	. . . euh . . .	Ach so! Ohwey!
Garn! Gerraway!	a ver. . .	Mais, non!	Ja! Los!
Why no, man!	Bueno . . .	Oh là là là là là!	Na, so was!
Naah!	¡Ojalá!	Zut alors!	Ach wo! Wie bitte?
. . . you know		Tu penses!	Blöd!
. . . look you!		J'en ai marre!	Meinst du?

THE CULTURAL DIMENSION OF VOCABULARY

The cultural dimension of vocabulary study is an area which teachers may wish to explore with their students from time to time.

The Harris report, which preceded the National Curriculum, pointed out that without a growing awareness of the **culture** of the target language speakers 'comprehension of **even basic words** may be partial or approximate'. What is meant by the cultural content of words is the connotations that words have for a particular group of people, and it is by exploring these connotations that students can begin to appreciate the cultural aspect of vocabulary.

There are three main approaches to teaching students how to investigate connotations and to compare them with what appear to be the same words in their own language.

WORD ASSOCIATIONS

English students are asked to write down in a 'spidergram' all that comes into their minds when they hear or see particular words. They then compare their spidergrams with each other and then do a further investigation by looking up the definitions of the words in a bilingual dictionary. TL students do the same with the 'equivalent' words and the results are exchanged and a comparative study is made, looking at the words in a variety of contexts.

The words which were used as examples for the post-16 students were 'private' and 'public'/'*privat*' and '*öffentlich*'. At a slightly lower level such words as the following might be appropriate words to explore in the same way:

English	*Español*	*Français*	*Deutsch*
Cheese	Queso	Fromage	Käse
Bread	Pan	Pain	Brot
Family	Familia	Famille	Familie
School	Colegio	Ecole	Schule

ASKING AND LISTENING

Other ways of teaching students methods for investigating the cultural aspect of vocabulary are any one or a combination of the following techniques:

CiLT

- a systematic series of interviews with TL speakers about particular words, with the questions being designed to elicit connotations;
- a group interview with TL speakers where they discuss a particular word and what it means to them;
- a series of notes enumerating how the investigator has heard or seen a word used.

CORPUS LINGUISTICS

The technique of this field of study is to build very large data banks of words in their contexts. The data in the Bank of English, for example, is composed of fifty million words from written texts and ten million words of transcribed speech. Words from this database can be looked up on the Internet (www.cobuild.collins.co.uk) and new Collins dictionaries are now based on this *corpus*. When a word is looked up it is quoted with a few words to each side and a perusal of these phrase groups helps the learner to appreciate the contexts and associations of the words. The illustration below (*Figure 4*) is drawn from the 40 lines displayed when the preposition 'above' is looked up.

Figure 4

warning to the enthusiastic Gemelli:	above	all 'he should avoid all value-
advanced level students aged 16 and	above,	and professional dancers.
Baitsbite roach nets to 13 lb	above	and below the lock.
. . . the horses drawn number nine and	above	are invariably pushed towards the . . .
The net monthly payments quoted	above	assume tax relief at 25% has been . . .
. . . was being formed to carry out legal,	above-	board trading activities . . .
and, indeed, he has been all the	above,	but he is also one of the most . . .
trip to the sort of places mentioned	above	can be the trip of a lifetime.
. . . to that 'spirit of freedom' mentioned	above,	'interior mortification' . . .
. . .crawled forward, a few hundred feet	above	Inverness-shire. We were almost on . .
with Ch'i the Banner and appears	above	it, the army will be defeated, a . . .
and Island Helicopter for tours	above	Manhattan. Sit back and relax as
However, as I briefly indicated	above	(page 93), it is not necessarily
words that do not conform to the	above	rules have a written accent over
Aberdeenshire. bachelor Edward,	above,	takes the leading role from today
assume a speed limit ten per cent	above	that assumed by the Department of
were found at ground zero, directly	above	the bomb lying in a shaft 1900 feet
only when I saw his great head look	above	the overhang that I realised my
hands clamped around his leg inches	above	the bloodstained bandage covering
view that his own genius raised him	above	the common stock, yet who demanded
on Europe or anything else,	above	the overriding need to defeat
eavesdropping to do as he sat	above	the courtyard pretending to read
wheelchair, legs amputated six inches	above	the knees. Snoot and Frouncy's boy . . .
immigrant groups have typically risen	above	the average incomes and . . .
that a black had uttered a thought	above	the level of plain narration; never . . .
boots for both riding and walking.	above	them, either a flannel shirt or . . .
silhouetted on the mountainside	Above	them. Dressed in olive-green . . .
And as you see, if you look around	above	us, hanging from the ceiling, there
Whoosh, one tackle is just	above	waist high.

Although this is a fairly new field, it is potentially a fascinating way of getting to the meaning beneath the surface of words. On a more modest scale, advanced learners could find this a useful way of investigating the essence of words by making their own collection of common words in context as in *Figure 4*.

10. Helping pupils to help themselves

An aspect of teaching which is easy to forget is telling pupils **why** they are doing things. Learners of any age do need to have confidence that their teachers know what they are doing and telling them the reasons why they are doing particular activities (a particular homework or test, the reason for playing a game, etc.) can be a motivating factor in their learning.

It may be worth considering giving them an occasional hand-out as a way of focusing their attention on matters which it can be too easily assumed that they know. *Figures 5 and 6* are suggestions for the form that tips for studying might take:

Figure 5

TIP OF THE DAY

Homework	Testing each other	Reading or listening
• Organise your evening into what you **have** to do and what you **want** to do • Make a quick time-table (don't forget to include your favourite TV programme or that game of football) • If your homework includes **learning,** put it into three ten-minutes slots, rather than one half hour • sit at a desk or table • give yourself a time limit • start with the hard things first • leave the music until you have a break in your work	• Spend a couple of minutes looking through the words to be tested • Get your partner to hide his or her list • Ask for the word in the way the teacher tells you • If the answer doesn't come immediately, supply the word and move on • After several more words, go back to the one s/he didn't know • and ask again **STOP** • Change roles **IF YOU WORK QUICKLY YOU WILL LEARN QUICKLY AND IT CAN BE FUN!**	• When we are learning a new language it has been discovered that the best way to enlarge your vocabulary is to read widely and listen to lots of people talking • What you have been given for homework should be interesting or enjoyable (or both!) • If you don't think it is, do it just the same. **Remember: this is the best way to build up enough new words to be able to understand this language.**

Figure 6

TIP OF THE DAY

Reading	Learning a list of words by heart	Speaking homework
• Glance quickly through the text, to try to work out what it's about (if there's a title, there'll probably be a clue or two in it) • Read fairly quickly, but pause at full-stops to check that you have the meaning (if not, read that bit again) • At the end read the whole text again • If there are words that are still puzzling you at this stage, look them up in the dictionary **RESIST THE TEMPTATION TO LOOK UP WORDS YOU DON'T KNOW TOO SOON!**	• Split the list into groups of three or four words • Learn each group separately • Test yourself (each group at a time) — be tough! • Test the whole list • Do something totally different • Test yourself again (mark those that you don't get right) • Do something else • Test yourself again • Get someone else to test you • Then, test someone else yourself, trying to rely on your memory to check whether they are right	• In class tomorrow you will be asked to give sentences, using each of the new words in your list • Don't write anything down • Think of your sentence • If you don't know how to say something, try to put it another way (don't be too ambitious) • If you really need a particular word that you don't know, look it up in the dictionary • Record your sentence • Listening to it and record it again if you're not satisfied • Now do the same with the other words in your list

USING THE POST-16 LEARNERS

The value of using pupils to create word-games for each other has already been mentioned. Using older learners to create materials for more junior pupils is also useful for both age groups.

Even when schools do not have their own sixth form they are usually connected to a post-16 institution. In the first few weeks of the post-GCSE course, one of the ways of 'bridging the gap' is to take the Areas of Experience C, D and E and study them from a more mature point of view. This is also the time when teachers need to make sure that advanced learners have the tools they will need (dictionary skills, knowledge of basic grammatical terminology, etc).

C*i*LT

It is during this period that a valid language task is for students to examine the vocabulary list for a particular topic in a junior course book and compare it with what is needed to achieve the specific goal set by the teacher. For example, they are shown the section in Chapter 1 of this book on 'Weather'. They are asked to select key-words for that task and list them according to the different parts of speech, saying whether they will be needed for receptive or productive use (another useful concept for them to think about at this stage). In this way, they are revising their own basic vocabulary and at the same time beginning to look at vocabulary analytically. In the process, they are ensuring that their grammatical terminology is in place. The result of this 'research' can then be used as the basis for vocabulary lists for younger learners, thus killing two birds with one stone.

The problem of finding sufficient continuous reading material for junior pupils can also be partly solved by asking for some creative writing from older pupils. They can be given a list of words from a specific part of a junior course and asked to weave a story round it. Alternatively, good material has sometimes come from giving older students a free rein.

The main thrust of this book has been to emphasise that the most effective and permanent vocabulary learning is the result of frequent exposure to a wide range of spoken and written language, supported by plenty of oral and written practice of an enjoyable and interesting kind. The most successful language learners are those who are not only motivated by the need to pass examinations but are also stimulated by imaginative and creative teaching and materials.

Appendix A   Satellite

The most useful satellite for those interested in foreign language television is Eutelsat (Hotbird I, Hotbird II) at (13° E), although if German is the only language required it is well served on the Astra satellite. Channels currently available for the main languages taught in this country are:

French   **TV5** — a selection of programmes, intended for Francophones living abroad, from the following :
CTQC   Consortium des Télévisions Québecoises et Canadiennes
RTBF   Radio-Télévision Belge Francophone
SRC   Société Radio-Canada
TF1   Télévision Française 1
TSR   Télévision Suisse-Romande
RFO   Radio-télévision Française d'outre-mer
La Cinquième — an educational programme sponsored by various French ministries. Usually short programmes aimed at French-speaking schools.
Arte — mainly documentary, news and 'art' films

Spanish   **RTEI** Radio-Televisión Española Internacional (2 programmes). Aimed at Spanish speakers abroad.

German   **VIVA/VIVA 2/ONYX** — music videos
RTL-2 — general entertainment
DEUTSCHE WELLE — mainly news and information, some documentaries (useful)
VOX (Austria) — news and entertainment (useful at times)

Italian   **Rai Uno, Rai Due, Rai Tre.** Mainly news and current affairs

EuroNews and **Eurosport** are available in English, French, German, Italian and Spanish.

Most companies transmitting on these satellites have no charges for receiving them, so the cost is limited to purchasing the parabola and the receiver/decoder.

The **radio programmes** currently available on the Hotbird satellites are: France Inter, France Culture, Radio Canada, Swiss Radio, Deutsch Welle, RNE (Radio exterior) RAI Internazionale, etc.

Other languages available from the same satellites are Arabic, Dutch, Polish and Portuguese

Other television programmes are transmitted from the same satellite which may be of interest to non-linguists. At the time of writing they include Eurosport, Euronews, a wild-life channel, financial and business news, various popular music videos (mainly German) and a non-stop fashion programme.

CiLT

Appendix B   Groupwork and pairwork

Frequent mention of pairwork has been made in this book. Since recent observation suggests that there is a tendency to abandon this mode of working, it is worth considering the reasons why it does not always work as well as it might.

The following disadvantages of **groupwork** are good reasons for only using it occasionally in highly controlled situations:

(i)   it is an invitation to waste time talking about other things;
(ii)   it creates an opportunity for disruptive behaviour;
(iii) most classrooms are too small for adequate privacy between groups;
(iv)   it involves moving furniture;
(v)   the more retiring pupils are not involved.

On the other hand, with **pairwork** it is much easier to overcome these problems and, provided that certain principles are followed, the advantages are worth the effort:

Pupils need training to go into the **pairwork mode** at frequent intervals during a lesson. It should not be seen as a special occasion, needing a lot of organisation.

They need a certain amount of initial training, when the procedure will be more important than the content. They need practice in these matters:
•   being quiet and business-like
•   working quickly
•   talking in the TL all the time
•   moving on to another task if they finish early
•   moving back to the *whole-class* mode immediately they are told

The teacher needs to:
•   set the task as briefly as possible, demonstrating with the help of a pupil rather than talking, and ignoring questions at this stage;
•   give them a time limit (two or three minutes is often ample);
•   watch to check that they begin immediately, naming those who do not do so;
•   answer individual questions;
•   avoid the temptation to get too involved with individuals;
•   continue to watch;
•   supply an extra task for those who finish early.

When classes can work with quick bursts of pairwork in this way it will be found to be not only a useful way of practising speaking, but also an invaluable way of teaching pupils how to co-operate with each other on **testing vocabulary**.

Appendix C   Creating your own listening materials

One of the ways of doing this is by using a foreign language assistant, or a group of assistants. It is unlikely that they will have done anything like this before, so it is worthwhile spending a little time before they begin a recording session drawing attention to a few points which will help you to get material which will be useful:

- The end product should sound **natural** and **unrehearsed.**
- Speak **slowly** and **clearly** but not as if you were reading.
- Try **not to distort** your natural pronunciation and intonation.
- Think about the **level** of the learner (e.g. KS3 or KS4).
- Plan first in your mind. **Avoid the temptation to write** (unless you want to jot down a few key words).

Material produced by the assistant(s) may be in the form of monologues, dialogues or discussions. *Figures 7–9* are suggestions about the sorts of things they can talk about, without too much difficulty. Recordings such as these will provide a rich source of material for classroom use and will be a way of building up a bank of material suitable for listening homework.

Figure 7: monologues

1   Talk about **where you live** in your home country/ in England (house/flat . . . old/new . . . where . . . number of bedrooms . . . other rooms . . . where you spend most of the time: indoors/ garden/balcony, etc).

2   Talk about what **you can/can't do** (speak Italian . . . play the piano . . . use a word processor . . . speak Japanese . . . type . . . swim . . . play tennis . . . ski . . . cook . . . draw, etc).

3   Talk about what **other members of your family can/ can't do.** (See list under 2.)

4   Talk about what **you/your family like** doing in your spare time. (What **you/they would do if** you/they won the lottery.)

5   A short history of your life.

6   What you have found **different** about your home town and where you live now. What you have found different about your own country and England. (Don't be frightened about mentioning **negative reactions as well as positive** reactions. Say what you find odd/unusual/surprising/ annoying.)

7   What **you are going to do** at Christmas/in the summer/during the next holidays. What you are going to do this weekend/next year, etc. And members of your family?

8   What you **did** during your last holiday/last weekend, etc.

9   What **it was like** when your grandparents **were** young.

Figure 8: dialogues and discussions

Two or three 'native speakers' get together and:

1   decide on the objective (where it will fit into the Scheme of Work);

2   look at the available vocabulary (perhaps by consulting a GCSE list of vocabulary);

3   produce a **scenario** (Where are you? . . . Who are you . . ? What are you discussing? . . . Who will take what angle?);

4   don't write anything down;

5   don't worry about slips of the tongue (that's the advantage of not using professional actors).

Another useful technique for collecting sound records is the interview with anybody who is available. Friends and acquaintances abroad can be pressed into service for this, or a group of exchange pupils can be taken to one side for a quick recording session. If this is a technique which teachers have not yet exploited, a few hints may be useful:

Figure 9: interviews

1   The interviewer should jot down a few key words and question forms (NB: if he or she writes down a whole series of questions it is unlikely that the result will sound natural and unrehearsed).

2   Think of questions which will encourage the other person to speak:
    NOT 'Do you . . . ' 'Are you . . . ' 'Have you', etc.
    BUT 'Tell me about . . . ', 'Why . . . ?' What was it like . . ?

3   Think of the use to which you hope to put the recording:
    (i)   for **reinforcement** of vocabulary, previously presented;
    (ii)   for the **presentation** of new vocabulary;
    (iii) for practising the use of specific **tenses** (future, past, conditional);
    (iv)   for providing opportunities for **extending vocabulary;**
    (v)   for **cultural** awareness (differences, similarities).

Material collected in the ways described above may be sometimes used for classroom presentation of new vocabulary but it is more likely to produce material for **gist listening**, which can be put on tapes and lent out for homework. It can also be placed in a listening library with self-access during 'quiet reading/listening' periods. If it is handled in this way, there does need to be some check that work set has been done, but it does not have to take the form of a written test with questions and answers! By asking pupils, just to tell you and the class about the content of a tape, they are learning to use new vocabulary for a **purpose** and incidentally reinforcing it. Teachers who have been able to find time to organise regular listening of this kind have been able to perceive a marked improvement in vocabulary acquisition.

Further reading

Gruneberg M M, *Linkword: Spanish in a day* (London: Corgi Books, 1994)

One of a series of Linkword books in various languages which develop the notion of learning vocabulary through association with a similar-sounding English words.

Hatch E and C Brown, *Vocabulary, Semantics, and Language Education* (Cambridge: University Press, 1995)

A comprehensive textbook prepared for an introductory course in linguistics at the University of California, Los Angleles. In addition to a complete study of the theories and research there are many practical suggestions for students of English.

McCarthy M, *Vocabulary* (Oxford: University Press, 1990)

A manual for teachers of English as a second language. Considers theoretical, descriptive, and psycholinguistic models of the vocabulary of English. Then offers many tasks for the teacher, designed to explore ways of translating theory into practice. Much of it applicable to MFL.

Nation P (ed), *New ways in teaching vocabulary* (Alexandria, Virginia, USA: Teachers of English to Speakers of Other Languages, 1994)

A TESOL handbook with contributions from teachers of English round the world. The activities are soundly based on well-tried principles. Many of the ideas are adaptable to MFL teaching.

Wenden A and J Ruben, *Learner strategies in language learning* (London: Prentice-Hall International, 1987)

A collection of contributions from teacher trainers and applied linguists on various aspects of language learning. From the point of view of the present volume, there are interesting chapters on mnemonic techniques for learning vocabulary and promoting learner autonomy.

CiLT